Introduction

A statue of Wheatley as part of Boston Women's Memorial

"The world is a severe schoolmaster, for its frowns are less dangerous than its smiles and flatteries, and it is a difficult task to keep in the path of wisdom." –

Phillis Wheatley has always been a difficult figure for people to wrap their minds around, both during her life and centuries after it. Indeed, she fits no easy stereotypes that historians or contemporaries liked to use to classify their subjects. Even her name is complicated, with her first name being spelled at times "Phyllis," and her surname being given without the extra "e" in the final syllable. Like so much of her life, her name was not the one given to her by her parents but instead by the people who first enslaved her. In the same vein, she was married, but for such a short time that her husband's surname never fully attached to her own.

Then there was the matter of her "career," which has always escaped definition. In the 18th century, enslaved people were not supposed to have been educated, certainly not to the level that Wheatley was, nor were they supposed to have creative abilities beyond those taught to them by their masters. In a time and place where slaves were rarely taught to read, they were obviously not expected to write better poetry than the vast majority of their peers.

But if Wheatley refused to be placed in a box and labeled during her life, that has been even more the case after her death. Given that she was a child who was transported from Africa and raised in slavery, her poetry contains none of the sorrow or angst that modern readers would anticipate seeing. In fact, in one of her most controversial works, "On being brought from Africa to America," she wrote:

> "'Twas mercy brought me from my Pagan land,
> Taught my benighted soul to understand
> That there's a God, that there's a Saviour too:
> Once I redemption neither sought nor knew.
> Some view our sable race with scornful eye,
> 'Their colour is a diabolic dye.'
> Remember, Christians, Negroes, black as Cain,
> May be refin'd, and join th' angelic train."

This can seem disconcerting, but it is also in keeping with other Christian literature through the ages in that it points to something terrible being used by God to bring about conversion and salvation. In that sense, it is not so much a defense of slavery, as some would interpret it, as it is a glorification of grace that could overcome tragedy. Her work may also have been influenced by the fact that Wheatley's experience of slavery was an abbreviated one, as she received her freedom upon adulthood.

In the end, Wheatley's freedom and abilities failed to yield the benefits that she no doubt desired. Her genius stifled under the pressure to make her own way in the world, and she ultimately died a pauper, but she remains one of the most unique and celebrated figures of the 13 colonies. *Phillis Wheatley: The Life and Legacy of the Slave Who Became Colonial America's Most Famous Poet* examines Wheatley's turbulent life and career. Along with pictures depicting important people, places, and events, you will learn about Phillis Wheatley like never before.

Early Years

"In every human Beast, God has implanted a Principle, which we call Love of Freedom; it is impatient of Oppression, and pants for Deliverance." – Phillis Wheatley

Given the circumstances of her birth, there can be little known for certain about Phillis Wheatley's early life, including when she was born, but it is known she lived somewhere near the coast of West Africa in the dark days when slave ships regularly arrived in search of new human cargo. While Phillis was still young, probably around the age of 8, leaders from a rival tribe came to her village, likely under the cover of darkness, and captured as many of the men, women, and children that they could carry away. Wheatley was one of the unlucky ones who did not escape and was thus taken from the only home she had ever known and marched through the jungle to the coast, where her captors sold her to Peter Gwin, captain of the slave ship *Phillis*.

Once aboard the ship, Phillis and her fellow "passengers" were quickly hustled down into the ship's hold, still stinking of the blood, vomit, and excrement left behind by the people who had previously crossed the Atlantic in bondage. She remained trapped in the hold, likely in chains, for the weeks that the voyage to Boston took. She landed on the shores of New England on July 11, 1761, and, after remaining below decks for nearly a month, she was finally removed from the ship and marched in the bright summer sunlight to the upper deck, where she stood for hours in the burning heat while John Avery, a well-known slave dealer, saw her auctioned off to the highest bidder.

Due to its association with the Civil War, it is often overlooked that slavery existed everywhere in colonies during the mid-18th century. In New England, there were fewer slaves than in Virginia and the Carolinas, and slaves were mostly household servants rather than agricultural laborers on plantations, but Wheatley was no freer in Massachusetts than she would have been in Virginia.

That said, the fact she was enslaved in New England and not further south proved significant for her future. Indeed, it was at the slave auction itself that Wheatley's horror story ended up being less worse than it could have been, for Susanna Wheatley was there that day. Susanna had been sent by her husband, John, to buy a young woman to serve as a companion and personal servant for her. According to Margaretta Matilda Odell's *Memoir and Poems of Phillis Wheatley: A Native African and a Slave*, "She was purchased by Mr. John Wheatley, a respectable citizen of Boston. This gentleman, at the time of the purchase, was already the owner of several slaves; but the females in his possession were getting something beyond the active periods of life, and Mrs. Wheatley wished to obtain a young negress, with the view of training her up under her own eye, that she might, by gentle usage, secure to herself a faithful domestic in her old age. She visited the slave-market, that she might make a personal selection from the group of unfortunates offered for sale."

Susanna was in poor health, and she hoped that having someone young to keep her company during the day would improve her quality of life. Odell continued, "There she found several robust, healthy females, exhibited at the same time with Phillis, who was of a slender frame, and evidently suffering from change of climate. She was, however, the choice of the lady, who acknowledged herself influenced to this decision by the humble and modest demeanor and the interesting features of the little stranger. The poor, naked child, (for she had no other covering than a quantity of dirty carpet about her like a fillibeg) was taken home in the chaise of her mistress, and comfortably attired. She is supposed to have been about seven years old, at this time, from the circumstance of shedding her front teeth."

A Wheatley family member later wrote about the family's purchase of Phillis, "In or about the year 1761, a slave-ship arrived in Boston harbor, with a cargo of slaves. Aunt Wheatley was in want of a domestic. She went on board to purchase. In looking through the ship's company of living freight, her attention was drawn to that of a slender, frail, female child, which at once enlisted her sympathies. Owing to the frailty of the child, she procured her for a trifle, as the captain had fears of her dropping off his hands, without emolument, by death."

Thus, the young child was bought and then taken by these strangers to their home on King Street. Once there, she was turned over to one of the female slaves to be cleaned up and dressed in a manner suitable for a servant living in a wealthy Bostonian family. Thankful to at least see people who looked like her, young Phillis, named after the ship that brought her to the colonies, began to look around and evaluate her new home. Communication, even with the other slaves, was difficult, but her youth and intelligence were on her side, and she soon began picking up some broken English.

As she settled into her new surroundings, Phillis was no doubt amazed by the frantic comings and goings outside her window, as King Street was a frenetic business center in colonial Boston, housing several printing and publishing houses, as well as bookstores. In time, Phillis came to learn that the Wheatley's were well-respected pillars of the Boston community and leading members of the New South Congregational Church. John Wheatley ran a profitable wholesale business and invested his profits wisely in real estate, which was a burgeoning business in colonial Boston as new people were constantly arriving in the city looking for housing. In addition to residential real estate, John also owned a number of warehouses along the docks and a ship named the *London Packet*.

The Old South Meeting House, where Phillis and the Wheatley family attended church

For her part, Susanna Wheatley devoted much of her time to reading, favoring religious books and the writings of the famous Calvinist preacher

George Whitefield. Though Whitefield was himself a Methodist, she found much to admire in his teachings and willingly donated both her time and money to his missionary work. She also regularly hosted some of the leading ministers of the day in her home, exposing young Phillis to some of the richest theological thought of the day.

John Russell's depiction of Whitefield

A Burgeoning Poet

"Some view our sable race with scornful eye,

"Their colour is a diabolic die."

Remember, Christians, Negroes, black as Cain,

May be refin'd, and join th' angelic train." – Phillis Wheatley

In the weeks that followed her arrival in the Wheatley home, Phillis met the young adults of the house, including 18-year-old twins Nathaniel and Mary. Nathaniel spent his days assisting his father and learning the family business, taking on more and more responsibility as he matured. Mary, on the other hand, enjoyed the life of an upper-middle-class young woman, attending dances and teas, paying calls, and reading poetry. However, there was a deeper side to the Wheatleys' only daughter, and she soon took a shine to young Phillis, who became something of a protégé to her. Mary began by

teaching Phillis the tenets of the Christian faith, for her parents had raised her
to believe that it was the duty of all masters to make sure their slaves heard
and embraced the Christian gospel. Then, when she saw how quickly the girl
mastered the theological information she was offered, Mary began
teaching her to read and understand both English and Latin literature. Mary
also schooled Phillis in ancient and modern history and geography, soon
giving the young slave a better education than most of the free women of the
city enjoyed.

According to author Harold Bloom, "Apparently she became well
acquainted with the Bible and with works of Horace, Vergil, Ovid, Terence,
and various contemporary English poets, especially Pope (and through his
translations, Homer), and probably Milton. Apparently, hers was an
education that would have been prized in many a Boston family, even among
its elite; and it was supplemented by contact with persons of status and
education, both townspeople and visitors, particularly ministers, who tended
to encourage her religious, intellectual, and literary development, apparently
sometimes sharing their books with her and occasionally even giving her
books to be her own."

Moreover, Wheatley lived in a place that would prove to be at the forefront
of colonial life in America, which bolstered Mary's teachings. Bloom
continued, "The location of the Wheatley home also provided another
education, one about much that was going on in Boston, certainly a leading
cultural and business center, experiencing growing friction with the British.
From this house she would witness or easily hear much about many of the
significant prerevolutionary actions of patriot protest and rebellion (and
British response) taking place nearby, and to some of them she responded
with early poems. However, despite various evidence in her poems and letters
of her sympathy and friendliness (for philosophical and personal reasons, as
well as because of local pride and business factors) with the patriots and with
the Revolution as it developed, she also maintained loyalist and British
friendships and contacts (for both personal and religious reasons)…[Phillis]
was young, black, female, a slave, a pious Christian, clever, talented, and
astute; and she understood the various aspects of her position in society and
the need to be alert, decorous, open, careful, and nimble of mind. She also
seems, above party and strife, to have been a loyal friend and a sincere
Christian. She was proud to be American in such trying times, but for her

there were many types of Americans--and, even more important, there were many types of Christians, all of them children of God, worthy of concern and help, and often capable of giving, and willing to give, help to her. Her principal loyalties were to God, herself, and the Wheatleys, in that order."

As a result, within just a few years of her arrival in America, Wheatley began writing poetry. John Wheatley himself later noted, "PHILLIS was brought from Africa to America, in the Year 1761, between Seven and Eight Years of Age. Without any Assistance from School Education, and by only what she was taught in the Family, she, in sixteen Months Time from her Arrival, attained the English Language, to which she was an utter Stranger before, to such a Degree, as to read any, the most difficult Parts of the Sacred Writings, to the great Astonishment of all who heard her. As to her WRITING, her own Curiosity led her to it; and this she learnt in so short a Time…. She has a great Inclination to learn the Latin Tongue, and has made some Progress in it. This Relation is given by her Master who bought her, and with whom she now lives."

Whether out of a sense of respect or paternalism, the Wheatley family soon came to support and even promote their slave's work. During a time when even most men could barely read and write, John and Susanna encouraged Phillis to expand her mind, going so far as to scale back her household assignments so that she would have more time and energy to pursue her craft. They also provided her ample firewood to keep a fire burning in her room throughout the night, and candles that could be lit at any time, for like so many other writers, she did some of her best work in the small hours of the morning. Furthermore, Phillis, having begun her life in the warm climes of Africa, never fully adjusted to New England's weather, so she had to take care lest she contract a cold. Indeed, having a fire in the middle of the night was a luxury the rest of the family did not enjoy; fires were put out in the evening after the home's occupants were tucked in under quilts and blankets.

Apparently, the Wheatley family's efforts paid large dividends in terms of loyalty and respect, for even as a very young woman, Wheatley was keenly aware of how unique her circumstances were, and she became grateful for the family's kind treatment. Of course, this was also canny on her part, given that the Wheatley family still held all the cards when it came to control over Phillis's life and agency. It was true that they their relationship with her evolved to the point that they invited her to accompany them to dinner parties held at the homes of friends, but they could just as easily take away all her books and writing materials and send her back to scrub pots in the kitchen. At the same time, it would be foolish to think the Wheatley's were wholly magnanimous when it came to how they dealt with Phillis, because they seemed to enjoy the notoriety that their association with the slave girl brought. For instance, in the case of dinner parties, their hosts likely broached the idea of bringing the slave who wrote poetry to the meal, not the other way around.

The first poem in Phillis's first book of poetry was entitled "On Messrs Hussey and Coffin." Wheatley had written it in 1765 after hearing a harrowing tale about two men, friends of the Wheatley family, who had nearly lost their lives at sea. It was published in Newport, Rhode Island, in December 1767:

> "Did Fear and Danger so perplex your Mind,
> As made you fearful of the Whistling Wind?
> Was it not Boreas knit his angry Brow
> Against you? or did Consideration bow?
> To lend you Aid, did not his Winds combine?
> To stop your passage with a churlish Line,
> Did haughty Eolus with Contempt look down
> With Aspect windy, and a study'd Frown?"

Emphasizing the Christian faith in which she had been instructed, Wheatley's poem provided an answer to the question it asked:

> "Regard them not; — the Great Supreme, the Wise,
> Intends for something hidden from our Eyes.
> Suppose the groundless Gulph had snatch'd away
> Hussey and Coffin to the raging Sea;
> Where wou'd they go? where wou'd be their Abode?
> With the supreme and independent God,
> Or made their Beds down in the Shades below,
> Where neither Pleasure nor Content can flow.
> To Heaven their Souls with eager Raptures soar,
> Enjoy the Bliss of him they wou'd adore.
> Had the soft gliding Streams of Grace been near,
> Some favourite Hope their fainting hearts to cheer,

Doubtless the Fear of Danger far had fled:
No more repeated Victory crown their Heads."

Then, she concluded, "Had I the Tongue of a Seraphim, how would I exalt thy Praise; thy Name as Incense to the Heavens should fly, and the Remembrance of thy Goodness to the shoreless Ocean of Beatitude! — Then should the Earth glow with seraphick Ardour. Blest Soul, which sees the Day while Light doth shine, To guide his Steps to trace the Mark divine."

When a member of the family (likely Susanna) sent the poem to the paper for publication, she added the following instructions: "Please to insert the following Lines, composed by a Negro Girl (belonging to one Mr. Wheatley of Boston) on the following Occasion, viz. Messrs Hussey and Coffin, as undermentioned, belonging to Nantucket, being bound from thence to Boston, narrowly escaped being cast away on Cape-Cod, in one of the late Storms; upon their Arrival, being at Mr. Wheatley's, and, while at Dinner, told of their narrow Escape, this Negro Girl at the same Time 'tending Table, heard the Relation, from which she composed the following Verses."

Having watched Phillis develop her talents, and having witnessed the girl's voracious thirst for knowledge, Susanna became determined to help her succeed, encouraging her to practice and refine her craft, as well as acting like something of a publicist when she felt the poems were worthy of publication. Tapping into her husband's business acquaintances, she was able to introduce the slave to people she would otherwise have never met. Susanna also raised funds to publish and print the poems, hoping that the public would find them appealing.

From the beginning, Wheatley's poems tended toward overtly Christian subjects, in keeping with the religious training she was receiving from the family. In 1767, "An Address To The Atheist, By P. Wheatley At The Age Of 14 Years" was published, and in it, Phillis wrote:

> "Muse! where shall I begin the spacious feild
> To tell what curses unbeleif doth yeild?
> Thou who dost daily feel his hand, and rod
> Darest thou deny the Essence of a God!--
> If there's no heav'n, ah! whither wilt thou go
> Make thy Ilysium in the shades below?

If there's no God from whom did all things Spring
He made the greatest and minutest Thing
Angelic ranks no less his Power display
Than the least mite scarce visible to Day
With vast astonishment my soul is struck
Have Reason'g powers thy darken'd breast forsook?"

In addition to cultivating Phillis's mind with a classical education, the family also exposed her to the increasing tensions between the colonists and England. Such was the teenager's interest in politics and current events that she wrote the following in 1769:

"To The King's Most Excellent Majesty On His Repealing The American Sta Act"

"Your Subjects hope
The crown upon your head may flourish long
And in great wars your royal arms be strong
May your Sceptre many nations sway
Resent it on them that dislike Obey
But how shall we exalt the British king

Who ruleth france Possessing every thing
The sweet remembrance of whose favours past
The meanest peasants bless the great the last
May George belov'd of all the nations round
Live and by earths and heavens blessings crownd
May heaven protect and Guard him from on high
And at his presence every evil fly
Thus every clime with equal gladness See
When kings do Smile it sets their Subjects free
When wars came on the proudest rebel fled
God thunder'd fury on their guilty head"

Wheatley completed one of her most famous poems not long after the death of the famous evangelist and leader of the Great Awakening, George Whitefield, in 1770:

"Hail happy Saint on thy immortal throne!

To thee complaints of grievance are unknown;
We hear no more the music of thy tongue,
Thy wonted auditories cease to throng.
Thy lessons in unequal'd accents flow'd!
While emulation in each bosom glow'd;
Thou didst, in strains of eloquence refin'd,
Inflame the soul, and captivate the mind.
Unhappy we, the setting Sun deplore!
Which once was splendid, but it shines no more;
He leaves this earth for Heaven's unmeasur'd height:
And worlds unknown, receive him from our sight;
There WHITEFIELD wings, with rapid course his way,
And sails to Zion, through vast seas of day.

  When his AMERICANS were burden'd sore,
When streets were crimson'd with their guiltless gore!
Unrival'd friendship in his breast now strove:
The fruit thereof was charity and love

  Towards America--couldst thou do more
Than leave thy native home, the British shore,
To cross the great Atlantic's wat'ry road,
To see America distress'd abode?
Thy prayers, great Saint, and thy incessant cries,
Have pierc'd the bosom of thy native skies!
Thou moon hast seen, and ye bright stars of light
Have witness been of his requests by night!
He pray'd that grace in every heart might dwell:
He long'd to see America excell;
He charg'd its youth to let the grace divine
Arise, and in their future actions shine;
He offer'd THAT he did himself receive,
A greater gift not GOD himself can give:
He urg'd the need of HIM to every one;
It was no less than GODS co-equal SON!"

  Take HIM ye wretched for your only good;
Take HIM ye starving souls to be your food.
Ye thirsty, come to his life giving stream:

Ye Preachers, take him for your joyful theme:
Take HIM, "my dear AMERICANS," he said,
Be your complaints in his kind bosom laid:
Take HIM ye Africans, he longs for you;
Impartial SAVIOUR, is his title due;
If you will clause to walk in grace's road,
You shall be sons, and kings, and priests to GOD."

With an irony lost on most of her readers, the slave girl regularly wrote poems supporting the American desire for freedom from England.

On February 22, 1770, a group of teenagers began throwing stones and rocks at the home of British customs official Ebenezer Richardson, who tried to disperse the teens by firing a shot to scare the crowd. Instead, the bullet mortally wounded a teenager named Christopher Seider, who was accorded a full funeral procession through Boston arranged by Samuel Adams himself. Richardson was subsequently convicted of murder but received a royal pardon and was allowed to continue working as a customs official, while Wheatley immortalized the boy in a poem titled, "On the Death of Mr. Snider Murder'd by Richardson."

"In heavens eternal court it was decreed
Thou the first martyr for the common good
Long hid before, a vile infernal here
Prevents Achilles in his mid career
Where'er this fury darts his Pois'nous breath
All are endanger'd to the shafts of death
The generous Sires beheld the fatal wound
Saw their young champion gasping on the ground
They rais'd him up but to each present ear
What martial glories did his tongue declare
The wretch appal'd no longer can despise
But from the Striking victim turns his eyes—
When this young martial genius did appear
The Tory chief no longer could forbear.
Ripe for destruction, see the wretches doom
He waits the curses of the age to come
In vain he flies, by Justice Swiftly chaced
With unexpected infamy disgraced

By Richardson for ever banish'd here
The grand Usurpers bravely vaunted Heir.
We bring the body from the watry bower
To lodge it where it shall remove no more
Snider behold with what Majestic Love
The Illustrious retinue begins to move
With Secret rage fair freedom's foes beneath
See in thy corse ev'n Majesty in Death."

Seider's death heightened tensions across the city, and on the evening of March 5, another teenager insulted a British officer regarding an overdue payment owed to the shop he was an apprentice at. British soldier Private Hugh White, who was standing guard outside the Custom house on King Street, told the teenager to be more respectful. When the teenager began insulting White, White struck him across the head with the butt of his musket.

Infuriated by White's assault, a larger group of Bostonians began crowding White and threatening him as he took up a defensive position on the steps of the Custom house. A handful of British soldiers, bayonets fixed, marched to the Custom house to protect White, and these soldiers found themselves confronted by a mob of hundreds of Bostonians taunting the soldiers and throwing snowballs at them. When one object hit British soldier Private Montgomery, he got back to his feet, shouted, "Damn you, fire!" and fired into the crowd, stunning everyone and nearly killing his own Captain, Thomas Preston. With that, several British soldiers began firing into the crowd as well, despite not being ordered to, killing or mortally wounding five people.

The site of the Boston Massacre is marked today by a circle in front of the State House

Having taken place on King Street, the Boston Massacre occurred near the Wheatley family's home, likely close enough that Phillis and the other family members could hear the shots being fired. A week later, the *Boston Evening Post* published Wheatley's poetic account of the event.

> "With Fire enwrapt, surcharged with sudden Death,
> Lo, the pois'd Tube convolves it's fatal Breath!
> The flying Ball with heav'n-directed Force.
> Rids the free Spirit of it's fallen Corse.
> Well fated Shades! let no unmanly Tear
> From Pity's Eye, distain your honour'd Bier:
> Lost to their View, surviving Friends may mourn,
> Yet o'er thy Pile shall Flames celestial burn;
> Long as in Freedom's Cause the Wise contend.
> Dear to your Country shall your Fame extend;
> While to the World, the letter'd Stone shall tell,
> How Caldwell, Attucks, Grey and Mav'rick fell."

It should be noted that the Wheatley family's interest in Phillis was not purely intellectual, for, like many of their generation, they considered the spiritual lives of their slaves to be their responsibility. That is how Phillis came to be taught not just about Homer and syntax, but also the tenets of the Christian faith, and that portion of her education reached its fruition on August 18, 1771, when she was baptized into membership of the Congregationalist Old South Church. One of the oldest churches in the colonies, it boasted among its members such illustrious figures as Samuel Adams, and Benjamin Franklin. It was from there, just two years later, that the former would signal the beginning of the Boson Tea Party.

By this time, the Wheatley family had become discouraged by how slowly American publishers were moving when it came to publishing Phillis's poems, so they began to market their slave's poems in England. According to Jacquelyn McLendon, author of *Phillis Wheatley: A Revoluitionary Poet*, "Susannah Wheatley enlisted the aid of Captain Robert Calef to help get the book published in London. Calef was a Wheatley family friend and the commander of the Wheatleys' ship, the London Packet, which sailed regularly between Boston and London. …Calef contacted Archibald Bell, a London Bookseller, who accepted the book for publication. Calef and Bell sought permission to dedicate the book to the countess of Huntingdon. The appearance of her name in the book would help to increase its recognition and its sales."

Selina Hastings, the Countess of Huntingdon, was a good choice for sponsorship. Decades earlier in 1739, at the age of 32, she underwent a religious conversion that led her to become active in the Methodist movement then spreading through England and America. Sometime around the middle of the 18th century, she established "The Countess of Huntingdon's Connection," a center for studying and advancing Methodism.

Hastings

Wheatley had previously flattered the Countess by mentioning her in a memorial poem to George Whitefield, in which she wrote:

> "Great COUNTESS! we Americans revere
> Thy name, and thus condole thy grief sincere:
> We mourn with thee, that TOMB obscurely plac'd,
> In which thy Chaplain undisturb'd doth rest.
> New-England sure, doth feel the ORPHAN's smart;
> Reveals the true sensations of his heart:
> Since this fair Sun, withdraws his golden rays,
> No more to brighten these distressful days!"

The Countess' Christian faith was all the connection the Wheatley family needed to make her acquaintance. Susanna wrote to a reverend, "Mr. Bell (the printer) Acquaints me that about 5 weeks ago he waited upon the Countess of Huntingdon with the Poems, who was greatly pleas'd with them, and pray'd him to Read them; and often would break in upon him and Say, 'is not this, or that, very fine? do read another,' and then expressd herself, She found her heart to knit with her and Questiond him much, whether She was Real without a deception? He then Convinc'd her by bringing my Name [Calef] in question. She is expected in Town in a Short time when we are both to wait upon her. I had like to forget to mention to you She is fond of having the Book Dedicated to her; but one thing She desir'd which She Said She hardly tho't would be denied her, that was to have Phillis' picture in the frontispiece. So that, if you would get it done it can be Engrav'd here, I do imagine it can be Easily done, and think would contribute greatly to the Sale of the Book. I am impatient to hear what the Old Countess Says upon the Occasion, & shall take the Earliest Opp,y of waiting upon her when She comes to Town."

There were men and women on both sides of the Atlantic who were sufficiently impressed with Wheatley's poetry to want to see it published. One anonymous woman wrote to the editor of the *London Magazine*, "SIR, As your Magazine is a proper repository for anything valuable or curious, I hope you will excuse the communicating the following by one of your subscribers. There is in this town a young Negro woman, who left her country at ten years of age, and has been in this eight years. She is a compleat sempstress, an accomplished mistress of her pen, and discovers a most surprising genius. Some of her productions have seen the light, among which is a poem on the death of the Rev. Mr. George Whitefield…The following was occasioned by her being in company with some young ladies of family, when one of them said she did not remember, among all the poetical pieces she had seen, ever to have met with a poem upon RECOLLECTION. The African (so let me calll; her, for so in fact she is) took the hint, went home to her master's, and soon sent what follows."

In responding to the proposal, Wheatley wrote, "MADAM, Agreeable to your proposing Recollection as a subject proper for me to write upon, I enclose these few thoughts upon it; and, as you was the first person who mentioned it, I thought none more proper to dedicate it to; and, if it meets with your approbation, the poem is honoured, and the authoress satisfied."

The poem, among the longest ever written by Wheatley, reflected the adolescent angst she felt as she stood on the brink of adulthood. It includes the following moving lines:

"And Thine the tribute of my youthful lays.
Now eighteen years their destin'd course have run,

In due succession, round the central sun;
How did each folly unregarded pass!
But sure 'tis graven on eternal brass!
To recollect, inglorious I return;
'Tis mine past follies and past crimes to mourn.
The virtue, ah! unequal to the vice,
Will scarce afford small reason to rejoice.
Such, RECOLLECTION! is thy pow'r, high-thron'd
In ev'ry breast of mortals, ever own'd.
The wretch, who dar'd the vengeance of the skies,
At last awakes with horror and surprise.
By Thee alarm'd, he sees impending fate,
He howls in anguish, and repents too late.
But oft thy kindness moves with timely fear
The furious rebel in his mad career.
Thrice bless'd the man, who in thy sacred shrine
Improves the REFUGE from the wrath divine."

By this time, there were many in Massachusetts who had heard of the girl and her poetry. Richard Cary, one of the colony's leading citizens, wrote to the Countess in May 1772, "The Negro Girl of Mr. Wheatley's, by her virtuous Behaviour and Conversation in Life gives Reason to believe, she's a Subject of Divine Grace--remarkable for her Piety, of an extraordinary Genius, and in full Communion with one of the Churches; the Family, & Girl, was Affected at the kind enquiry your Ladyship made after her."

As Wheatley's work expanded, so did her notoriety, and in October 1772, British businessman Thomas Wooldridge traveled to Boston from his home in St. Augustine. During his visit, he met Wheatley, and he subsequently wrote to an associate, "While in Boston, I heard of a very extraordinary female slave, who had made some verses on our mutually dear deceased Friend [Rev. George Whitefield]; I visited her mistress, and found by conversing with the African, that she was no Impostor: I asked if she could write on any Subject; she said Yes; we had just heard of your Lordship's appointment; I gave her your name, which she was acquainted with. She immediately wrote a rough Copy of the inclosed Address & Letter, which I promised to convey or deliver. I was astonished, and could hardly believe my own Eyes. I was present while she wrote and can attest that it is her own production; she shewed me her Letter to Lady Huntingdon, which I daresay, Your Lordship has seen; I send you an account signed by her master of her Importation, Education &c. they are all wrote in her own hand."

By this time, Wheatley had caught the attention of William, the Earl of Dartmouth, then King George III's Secretary of State for the North America. She honored him with one of her works, writing:

> "While you, my Lord, read o'er th' advent'rous Song
> And wonder whence Such daring boldness Sprung:
> Hence, flow my wishes for the common good
> By feeling hearts alone, best understood.
>
> ...
>
> May heav'nly grace, the Sacred Sanction give
>
> To all thy works, and thou for ever live,
> Not only on the wing of fleeting Fame,
> (Immortal Honours grace the Patriots' name!)
> Thee to conduct to Heav'ns refulgent fane;
> May feiry coursers sweep th' ethereal plain!
> Thou, like the Prophet, find the bright abode
> Where dwells thy Sire, the Everlasting God."

This poem is unusual in that it marks one of the few occasions Wheatley complained about her own enslavement. At the same time, she used this complaint to plead for the freedom of those who still held her in slavery:

> "From Native clime, when Seeming cruel fate
> Me snatch'd from Afric's fancy'd happy Seat
> Impetuous.-----Ah! what bitter pangs molest
> What Sorrows labour'd in the Parent breast!
> That more than Stone, ne'er Soft compassion mov'd
> Who from its Father Seiz'd his much belov'd.
> Such once my case.--Thus I deplore the day
> When Britons weep beneath Tyrannic sway.
> To thee, our thanks for favours past are due,
> To thee, we still Solicite for the new;
> Since in thy pow'r as in thy Will before,

To Sooth the griefs which thou didst then deplore."

In spite of Woodridge's praise, as well as that of others, before Wheatley's poems could be considered for publication in London, she had to endure an unusual educational examination. She was, after all, an African teenager then being held in slavery. Needless to say, each of those aspects was enough to make people suspicious, so the meeting was designed to serve a positive, if insulting, purpose. Speaking of this event, Professor Henry Louis Gates, Jr., painted this vivid picture: "On October 8, 1772, a small, delicate African woman, about eighteen years of age, walks into a room, perhaps in Boston's Town Hall, the Old Colony House, to be interviewed by eighteen gentlemen so august that they could later allow themselves to be identified publicly 'as the most respectable characters in Boston.' No doubt the young woman would have been demure, soft-spoken, and frightened, for she was about to undergo one of the oddest oral examinations on record, one that would determine the course of her life and the fate and direction of her work, and one that, ultimately, would determine whether she remained a slave or would be set free. The stakes, in other words, were as high as they could get for an oral exam. They had one simple charge: to determine whether Phillis Wheatley was truly the author of the poems she claimed to have written."

Gates continued, "She would have been familiar with the names of the gentlemen assembled in this room. For there, perhaps gathered in a semicircle, would have sat an astonishingly influential group of the colony's citizens determined to satisfy for themselves, and thus put to rest, fundamental questions about the authenticity of this woman's literary achievements. Their interrogation of this witness, and her answers, would determine not only this woman's fate, but the subsequent direction of the antislavery movement, as well as the birth of what a later commentator would call "a new species of literature," the literature written by slaves."

In explaining why this examination was critical not only to Wheatley herself but to the dialogue surrounding slavery in America and around the world, Gates noted, "If she had indeed written her own poems, then this would demonstrate that Africans were human beings and should be liberated from slavery. If, on the other hand, she had not written, or could not write her poems, or if indeed she was like a parrot who speaks a few words plainly, then that would be another matter entirely. Essentially, she was auditioning for the humanity of the entire African people. And so the bold gambit in the

Old Colony House--the decision to assemble some of the finest minds in all colonial America to question closely the African adolescent about the slender sheaf of twenty-eight poems that she and her master and mistress claimed that she had written by herself."

It is a credit not just to Wheatley's intellect, but also to her poise under pressure, that she passed her test and so impressed her examiners that they wrote, "We whose Names are under-written, do assure the World, that the Poems specified in the following Page, were (as we verily believe) written by Phillis, a young Negro Girl, who was but a few Years since, brought an uncultivated Barbarian from Africa, and has ever since been, and now is, under the Disadvantage of serving as a Slave in a Family in this Town. She has been examined by some of the best judges, and is thought qualified to write them."

When Wheatley's poetry was finally published, the words of her examiners created a special type of forward: "AS it has been repeatedly suggested to the Publisher, by Persons, who have seen the Manuscript, that Numbers would be ready to suspect they were not really the Writings of PHILLIS, he has procured the following Attestation, from the most respectable Characters in Boston, that none might have the least Ground for disputing their Original. WE whose Names are under-written, do assure the World, that the POEMS specified in the following Page, were (as we verily believe) written by PHILLIS, a young Negro Girl, who was but a few Years since, brought an uncultivated Barbarian from Africa, and has ever since been, and now is, under the Disadvantage of serving as a Slave in a Family in this Town. She has been examined by some of the best Judges, and is thought qualified to write them.

   His Excellency THOMAS HUTCHINSON, Governor,
The Hon. ANDREW OLIVER, Lieutenant-Governor.
The Hon. Thomas Hubbard,
The Hon. John Erving,
The Hon. James Pitts,
The Hon. Harrison Gray,
The Hon. James Bowdoin,
John Hancock, Esq;
Joseph Green, Esq;
Richard Carey, Esq;

The Rev. Charles Chauncey, D.D.
The Rev. Mather Byles, D.D.
The Rev. Ed. Pemberton, D.D.
The Rev. Andrew Elliot, D.D.
The Rev. Samuel Cooper, D.D.
The Rev. Mr. Saumel Mather,
The Rev. Mr. John Moorhead,
Mr. John Wheatley, her Master"

The introduction to the book read, "THE FOLLOWING POEMS were written originally for the Amusement of the Author, as they were the Products of her leisure Moments. She had no Intention ever to have published them; nor would they now have made their Appearance, but at the Importunity of many of her best, and most generous Friends; to whom she considers herself, as under the greatest Obligations. As her Attempts in Poetry are now sent into the World, it is hoped the Critic will not severely censure their Defects; and we presume they have too much Merit to be cast aside with Contempt, as worthless and trifling Effusions. As to the Disadvantages she has laboured under, with Regard to Learning, nothing needs to be offered, as her Master's Letter in the following Page will sufficiently show the Difficulties in this Respect she had to encounter. With all their Imperfections, the Poems are now humbly submitted to the Perusal of the Public."

In late February 1773, John Andrews preordered a copy of the book of poetry and wrote excitedly to his brother-in-law, "In regard to Phillis's poems they will originate from a London press, as she was blamd by her friends for printg them here & made to expd a large emolument if she sent ye copy home, which induced her to remand yt of ye printer & dld [delivered] it Capt Calef, who could not sell it by reason of their not crediting ye performance to be by a Negro, since which, she has had a paper drawn up & signd by the Govr. Council, Ministers & most of ye people of note in this place, certifying the authenticity of it; which paper Capt Calef carried last fall, thefore [therefore] we may expect it in print…by the spring ships, it is supposed the Coppy will sell for £ 100 sterlg: have not as yet been able to procure a coppy of her dialogue with Mr Murry, if I do, will send it."

As mentioned above, the Countess of Huntingdon insisted that a portrait of Phillis be featured on the frontpiece of the book. To satisfy this demand, the Wheatley's hired Scipio Moorhead, an African-American artist who, like Phillis Wheatley, was making a name for himself in spite of being the enslaved servant of Reverend John Moorhead. The Wheatley's and the Moorhead's had long been friends, and when the Reverend Moorhead died, Phillis wrote of him:

> "With humble Gratitude he render'd Praise,
> To Him whose Spirit had inspir'd his Lays;
> To Him whose Guidance gave his Words to flow,
> Divine instruction, and the Balm of Wo:
> To you his Offspring, and his Church, be given,
> A triple Portion of his Thirst for Heaven;
> Such was the Prophet; we the Stroke deplore,
> Which let's us hear his warning Voice no more.
> But cease complaining, hush each murm'ring Tongue,
> Pursue the Example which inspires my Song.
> Let his Example in your Conduct shine;
>
> Own the afflicting Providence, divine;
> So shall bright Periods grace your joyful Days,
> And heavenly Anthems swell your Songs of Praise."

Sarah, Moorhead's wife, had taught Scipio to draw and paint, and his talent allowed him a certain amount of limited freedom. Upon seeing his work, Wheatley honored him by writing a poem, "To S. M. a young African Painter, on seeing his Works," which included the following praise:

> "When first thy pencil did those beauties give,
>
> And breathing figures learnt from thee to live,
>
> How did those prospects give my soul delight,
>
> A new creation rushing on my sight?
>
> Still, wond'rous youth! each noble path pursue;
>
> On deathless glories fix thine ardent view:
>
> Still may the painter's and the poet's fire,

To aid thy pencil and thy verse conspire!

And may the charms of each seraphic theme

Conduct thy footsteps to immortal fame!"

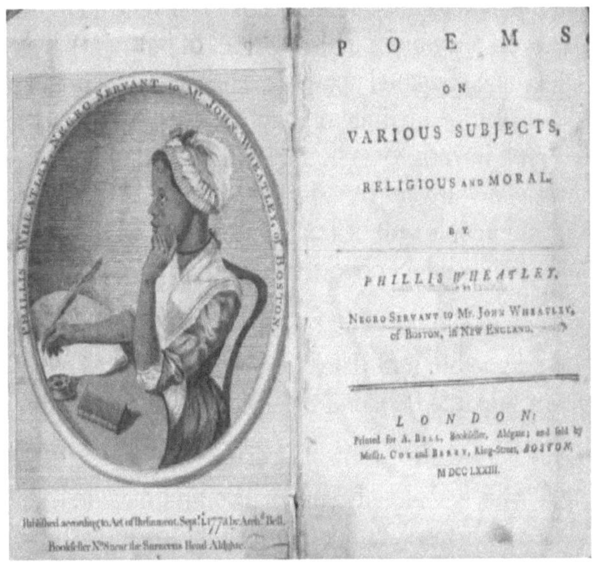

The frontpiece of the book

Freedom

Even as her work began to gain acclaim, Phillis's health had declined to the point that she often had to spend weeks away from Boston, recuperating in the fresh air of the surrounding countryside. In July 1772, she mentioned her difficulties while writing to Obour Tanner of New Port, Rhode Island, "I have been in a very poor state of health all the past winter and spring, and now reside in the country for the benefit of its more wholesome air. I came to town this morning to spend the Sabbath with my master and mistress...."

While Phillis was dealing with health issues, Mary Wheatley had married the Reverend John Lathrop and moved into a home of her own. Meanwhile, John Wheatley suffered a severe injury and retired from business, selling his remaining shares of his company to Nathaniel.

On March 29, 1773, Susanna Wheatley wrote to Samson Occom, a Presbyterian minister and the first Native American to have his writings published, "I wrote you before of the Sad accident which befel Mr. Wheatley from a fall, who remains in such a Situation, that he has never been able to get out of his Bed without the assistance of 5 or 6 men: and it is now near 5 weeks Since it happen'd. I am very weak and low, my old indispositions returning upon me, and to Such a degree, as makes me doubtful whether I shall live to See you once more in this World…I have rec'd a Letter from Capt Calef, he had waited upon Mr. Thornton but could not see him, therefore could not write anything upon our affairs; we expect him [Calef] every Day: My Son intends to go home [to England] with him. You Said you'd give him Letters to your freinds when he went. He would be glad as the roads are good and People will be travelling down this way You would Send them as Soon as a convenient opportunity presents."

Thus, when Nathaniel traveled to London in 1773, it was decided that Phillis should go with him. The two left Boston on May 8, sailing on the family's own ship, the *London Packet*, and they arrived six weeks later, on June 17.

By this time, Phillis had already shown a commitment to shaping her own destiny, and that of her work, rather than merely relying on others to make her successful. In April 1773, she placed the following advertisement in the *Massachusetts Gazette and the Boston News-Letter*:

PROPOSALS

For Printing in London by SUBSCRIPTION,
A Volume Of POEMS,
Dedicated by Permission to the Right Hon. the
Countess of Huntingdon.
Written by PHILLIS,
A Negro Servant to Mr. Wheatley of Boston
in New-England.

Terms of Subscription.

I. The Book to be neatly printed in 12 mo. on a new Type and a fine Paper, adorned with an elegant Frontispiece, representing the Author.
II. That the Price to Subscribers shall be Two Shillings Sewed or Two

Shillings and Six-pence neatly bound.

II. [sic] That every Subscriber deposit One Shilling at the Time of subscribing; and the Remainder to be paid on the Delivery of the Book.

Subscriptions are received by Cox & Berry, in Boston.

Once in London, Wheatley wrote to her benefactress, "It is with pleasure I acquaint your Ladyship of my safe arrival in London after a fine passage of 5 weeks, in the Ship London, with my young Master: (advis'd by my Physicians for my Health.) have Brought a letter from Richd. Carey Esqr. but was disappointed by your absence of the honour of waiting upon your Ladyship with it. I woud have inclos'd it, but was doubtful of the safety of the conveyance. I should think my self very happy in Seeing your Ladyship, and if you was So desirous of the Image of the Author as to propose it for a Frontispiece I flatter myself that you would accept the Reality I conclude with thanking your Ladyship for permitting the Dedication of my Poems to you; and am not insensible, that, under the patronage of your Ladyship, not more eminent in the Station of Life than in your examplary Piety and Virtue, my feeble efforts will be Shielded from the Severe trials of unpitying Criticism and, being encourag'd by your Ladyship's Indulgence, I the more freely resign to the world these Juvenile productions…"

Wheatley was also able to meet face-to-face with the men who would be publishing her poems. One of the most significant tasks she had to perform was to help them choose which poems would be included in the book. Obviously her most strident anti-British poetry would be left out. On the other hand, she was able to bring to them a new poem she had written during her voyage, "A Farewel to America."

"Adieu, New-England's smiling meads,

   Adieu, th' flow'ry plain:

I leave thine op'ning charms, O spring,

   And tempt the roaring main.

In vain for me the flow'rets rise,

   And boast their gaudy pride,

> While here beneath the northern skies
>
> I mourn for health deny'd.
>
> Celestial maid of rosy hue,
>
> Oh let me feel thy reign!
>
> I languish till thy face I view,
>
> Thy vanish'd joys regain."

Unfortunately, Wheatley was not able to remain in London long enough to see her book published, for that summer she and Nathaniel received word that Susanna was very ill. Concerned for the woman who had done so much for her, Wheatley returned to Boston on the next available ship. This was especially disappointing, since it meant that she had to miss her planned trip to visit the Countess of Huntingdon at her Welsh estate. She was also scheduled to be presented to King George III, another honor she had to forego.

Phillis left England alone in late July, Nathaniel having chosen to remain in London, and she arrived in Boston on September 13, just days after *Poems on Various Subjects, Religious and Moral* was released. The book seems to have made a bit of a splash in English literary circles, thanks in part to the publisher's support in the form of announcements and advertisements upon its release. At least six different bookstores in London alone carried the publication, not to mention other venues in England and Scotland.

As exciting as being a published author must have been for Wheatley, another event overshadowed it. Soon after she arrived back in Boston, the family informed Phillis that they were going to grant her freedom. The deed was accomplished by October 18 and, since she was now an adult, she was free to make her own decisions and enjoy the profits from her book.

Now responsible for her own future financial security, Phillis quickly went to work promoting her books. In addition to approaching literary leaders and bookstore owners personally, she also wrote a number of letters, including one to David Wooster around the time of her emancipation, in which she explained, "Since my return to America my Master, has at the desire of my friends in England given me my freedom. The Instrument is drawn, so as to secure me and my property from the hands of the Executrs. adminstrators, &c. of my master, & secure whatsoever should be given me as my Own…I expect my Books which are publishd in London in Capt. Hall, who will be here I believe in 8 or 10 days. I beg the favour that you would honour the enclos'd Proposals, & use your interest with Gentlemen & Ladies of your acquaintance to subscribe also, for the more subscribers there are, the more it will be for my advantage as I am to have half the sale of the Books, This I am the more solicitous for, as I am now upon my own footing and whatever I get by this is entirely mine, & it is the Chief I have to depend upon. I must also request you would desire the Printers in New Haven, not to reprint that Book, as it will be a great hurt to me, preventing any further Benefit that I might recieve from the Sale of my Copies from England."

The books did indeed arrive, and Wheatley wasted no time in reaching out to those who had shown interest in her efforts. She wrote to Reverend Samuel Hopkins in Newport, Rhode Island on February 9, "I take with pleasure this opportunity by the Post, to acquaint you of the arrl. of my books from London, I have Seal'd up a package, containing 17 for you 2 for Mr. Tanner and one for Mrs. Mason, and only wait for you to appoint some proper person by whom I may convey them to you, I recd. some time ago 20/sterling, upon them by the hands of your Son in a Letter from Obour Tanner; I recd. at the same time a paper by which I understood there are two Negro men who are desirous of returning to their native Country, to preach the Gospel; But being much indispos'd by the return of my Asthmatic complaint, besides, the sickness of my mistress who has been long confin'd to her bed, & is not expected to live a great while; all these things render it impracticable for me to do anything at present with regard to that paper. But what I can do in influencing my Christian friends and acquaintance, to promote this laudable design shall not be wanting."

These last words were significant, for from the time of her emancipation to the end of her life, there were some who pressured Wheatley to leave the only home she could remember and return to Africa as a missionary. This was a common theme among many of the early abolitionists who felt that the best thing to do for those brought from Africa against their will, and their descendants, was to return them to the land of their birth. While she obviously did not feel the need to return to Africa, she nonetheless shared her missioner friends' interest in the spiritual welfare of the continent: "My heart expanded, with sympathetic Joy, to see at distant time the thick cloud of ignorance dispersing from the face of my benighted Country…Africa is perishing with a Spiritual Famine. O that they could partake of the crumbs, the precious crumbs, Which fall from the table, of these distinguishd children of the Kingdome. Their minds are unprejudiced against the truth therefore tis to be hoped they woud. recieve it with their Whole heart, I hope that which the divine royal Psalmist Says by inspiration is now on the point of being Accomplish'd, namely. Ethiopia Shall Soon Stretch forth her hands Unto God, of this Obour Tanner (and I trust many others within your knowledge[)] are living witnesses…."

One of the things that so many proponents of the re-settlement option failed to realize about former slaves is that they were as American as those who had either been born in the colonies or come there as young children. Wheatley herself tried to convey this point tactfully to John Thornton, a London merchant who not only wanted her to go to Africa as a missionary, but also to marry one of the single men already assigned to that land. She wrote to him in May 1774, "You propose my returning to Africa with Bristol Yamma and John Quamine if either of them upon Strict enquiry is Such, as I dare give my heart and hand to, I believe they are either of them good enough if not too good for me, or they would not be fit for missionaries; but why do you hon'd Sir, wish those poor men so much trouble as to carry me So long a voyage? Upon my arrival, how like a Barbarian Shoud I look to the Natives; I can promise that my tongue shall be quiet for a strong reason indeed being an utter stranger to the Language of Anamaboe."

She then added, "This undertaking appears too hazardous, and not sufficiently Eligible, to go--and leave my British & American Friends--I am also unacquainted with those Missionaries in Person. The reverend gentleman who unde[r][ta]kes their Education has repeatedly informd. me by Letters of their pro[gress] in Learning also an Account of John Quamine's family and Kingdo[m] But be that as it will I resign it all to God's all wise governance; I thank you heartily for your generous Offer."

Instead of focusing exclusively on Africans, Wheatley used the power of her pen to cry out on behalf of the thousands of men and women who were still be held in bondage in America. In fact, that same month, she wrote a letter to Reverend Samson Occom that was published in part: "I have this Day received your obliging kind Epistle, and am greatly satisfied with your Reasons respecting the Negroes, and think highly reasonable what you offer in Vindication of their natural Rights: Those that invade them cannot be insensible that the divine Light is chasing away the thick Darkness which broods over the Land of Africa; and the Chaos which has reign'd so long, is converting into beautiful Order, and [r]eveals more and more clearly, the glorious Dispensation of civil and religious Liberty, which are so inseparably united, that there is little or no Enjoyment of one without the other…in every human Breast, God has implanted a Principle, which we call Love of Freedom; it is impatient of Oppression, and pants for Deliverance; and by the Leave of our modern Egyptians I will assert, that the same Principle lives in us. God grant Deliverance in his own Way and Time, and get him honour upon all those whose Avarice impels them to countenance and help forward the Calamities of their fellow Creatures." Finally, "This I desire not for their Hurt, but to convince them of the strange Absurdity of their Conduct whose Words and Actions are so diametrically opposite. How well the Cry for Liberty, and the reverse Disposition for the exercise of oppressive Power over others agree,--I humbly think it does not require the Penetration of a Philosopher to determine."

Her writings and those of others of her generation laid the groundwork for the abolition movement that would reach its fruition a century later. In his article, "The Puritan Origins of Black Abolitionism in Massachusetts," published in the *Historical Journal of Massachusetts* in 2011, Christopher Cameron observed, "Among these abolitionists, none was better known than Phillis Wheatley, who reformulated Puritan religious ideas into a critique against slavery. Wheatley's poetry evinced the influence of Puritan covenant theology, a school of thought that came into being during the seventeenth century when Puritan leaders such as John Winthrop sought to explain the relationship of New England with God."

He continued, "In her poem 'On the Death of General Wooster,' Wheatley subtly employed covenant theology to argue against slavery, asking 'how, presumptuous shall we hope to find/Divine acceptance with th' Almighty mind–/While yet (O deed ungenerous!) they disgrace/And hold in bondage Afric's blameless race?' In these few lines Wheatley argued that

America would not be successful in the revolutionary war of the 1770s if it continued to enslave Blacks because this practice was immoral and a breach of New England's covenant with God. This would not be the case if Americans abolished slavery, she argued, telling the colonists to 'Let virtue reign—And thou accord our prayers/Be victory our's, and generous freedom theirs.' Once the colonists became virtuous enough to abolish slavery, according to Wheatley, they would achieve success in the war with Britain."

Though she was no longer bound to them as a slave, Phillis and the Wheatley's still shared ties of friendship and affection, and she made no immediate moves to go out on her own. Instead, she remained in the home in much the same manner she always had, with one remarkable difference: she knew she could leave, and so did the family. If anything, this made her devotion to the dying Susanna even sweeter, as Phillis nursed her through her final days until she died on March 3, 1774.

Susanna's death greatly pained Phillis, and she wrote about the loss to Obour Tanner, a family friend who had written to her ordering five copies of her book, on March 21, "I have lately met with a great trial in the death of my mistress, let us imagine the loss of a Parent, Sister or Brother the tenderness of all these were united in her.--I was a poor little outcast & a stranger when she took me in. not only into her house but I presently became, a sharer in her most tender affections, I was treated by her more like her child than her Servant, no opportunity was left unimprov'd, of giving me the best of advice, but in terms how tender! how engaging! this I hope ever to keep in remembrance. Her examplly life was a greater monitor than all her precepts and Instruction, thus we may observe of how much greater force example is than Instruction."

Following Susanna's death, Phillis still remained in the home, helping care for the bereaved John Wheatley, whose married children had their own lives to live and young families to care for. But even as she continued living the daily life of a beloved servant, Phillis's horizons were clearly wider than they had ever been before, as were her friendships and opportunities. Among her new friends was Mary Shubrick Eveleigh, the wife of Nicholas Eveleigh, the man destined to be the first Comptroller of the United States Treasury. After his death, she would go on to marry Edward Rutledge, a signer of the Declaration of Independence signer Edward Rutledge. Though a native of South Carolina, Eveleigh traveled through Massachusetts during the years leading up to the American Revolution and likely met Wheatley, as the latter gave her an autographed copy of her book of poetry. On September 24, 1774, Eveleigh presented Wheatley with a valuable gift of a number of beautifully bound volumes.

It was also during this period in her life that Wheatley entered into a public, poetic correspondence with an anonymous Royal Navy lieutenant. According to Mason, "Vice-Admiral Samuel Graves had become commander in chief of the North American station, at Boston, in the summer of 1774. A good many men in the Royal Navy in the eighteenth century, including Samuel Graves, had served along the coast of Africa because of the trading done by the English in the Senegambia and Gold Coast areas…. Apparently, the lieutenant of these poems was attached to Graves's command, may have seen service on the coast of Africa, and was an admirer of Milton and Newton."

In her first poem addressed to him, Wheatley wrote:

> "Far in the space where ancient Albion keeps
> Amidst the roarings of the sacred deeps,
> Where willing forests leave their native plain,
> Descend, and instant, plough the wat'ry main.
> Strange to relate! with canvas wings they speed
> To distant worlds; of distant worlds the dread.
> The trembling natives of the peaceful plain,
> Astonish'd view the heroes of the main,
> Wond'ring to see two chiefs of matchless grace,
> Of generous bosom, and ingenuous face,
> From ocean sprung, like ocean foes to rest,
> The thirst of glory burns each youthful breast."

To her subtle criticism of the British slave trade, the lieutenant replied:

> "Behold with reverence, and with joy adore;
> The lovely daughter of the Affric shore,
> Where every grace, and every virtue join,
> That kindles friendship and makes love divine;
> In hue as diff'rent as in souls above;
> The rest of mortals who in vain have strove,
> Th' immortal wreathe, the muse's gift to share,

Which heav'n reserv'd for this angelic fair.

  Blest be the guilded shore, the happy land,
Where spring and autumn gently hand in hand;
O'er shady forests that scarce know a bound,
In vivid blaze alternately dance round:
Where cancers torrid heat the soul inspires;

  With strains divine and true poetic fires;
(Far from the reach of Hudson's chilly bay)
Where cheerful phœbus makes all nature gay;
Where sweet refreshing breezes gently fan;
The flow'ry path, the ever verdent lawn,
The artless grottos, and the soft retreats;
"At once the lover and thee muse's seats."

Not to be outdone, Phillis responded with the following:

  "The heavenly sisters pour thy notes along
And crown their bard with every grace of song.
My pen, least favour'd by the tuneful nine,
Can never rival, never equal thine;
Then fix the humble Afric muse's seat

  At British Homer's and Sir Isaac's feet.
Those bards whose fame in deathless strains arise
Creation's boast, and fav'rites of the skies.

  In fair description are thy powers display'd
In artless grottos, and the sylvan shade;
Charm'd with thy painting, how my bosom burns!"

  Ultimately, she concluded,
And pleasing Gambia on my soul returns,
With native grace in spring's luxuriant reign,
Smiles the gay mead, and Eden blooms again,
The various bower, the tuneful flowing stream,
The soft retreats, the lovers golden dream,
Her soil spontaneous, yields exhaustless stores;
For phœbus revels on her verdant shores.

Whose flowery births, a fragrant train appear,
And crown the youth throughout the smiling year,

   There, as in Britain's favour'd isle, behold
The bending harvest ripen into gold!
Just are thy views of Afric's blissful plain,
On the warm limits of the land and main."

By this time, the animosity between the American colonists and the British were heating up to a near fevered level. On April 19, 1775, fighting at Lexington and Concord concluded with colonial militia laying siege to British forces in Boston. The start of the American Revolution compelled many to leave the city, including John Wheatley, who moved north to Chelsea. Mary and her husband also left, fleeing to Providence, Rhode Island, where Phillis joined them.

In October 1775, Phillis completed one of her most famous poems, addressed to the new leader of the Continental Army, George Washington. Capturing the colonists' trust in him, she wrote:

   "Celestial choir! enthron'd in realms of light,

Columbia's scenes of glorious toils I write.

While freedom's cause her anxious breast alarms,

She flashes dreadful in refulgent arms.

See mother earth her offspring's fate bemoan,

And nations gaze at scenes before unknown!

See the bright beams of heaven's revolving light

Involved in sorrows and the veil of night!"

Then, once again combining classical imagery with Christian principles, she continued:

   "The Goddess comes, she moves divinely fair,

Olive and laurel binds Her golden hair:

Wherever shines this native of the skies,

Unnumber'd charms and recent graces rise.

 Muse! Bow propitious while my pen relates

How pour her armies through a thousand gates,

As when Eolus heaven's fair face deforms,

Enwrapp'd in tempest and a night of storms;

Astonish'd ocean feels the wild uproar,

The refluent surges beat the sounding shore;

Or think as leaves in Autumn's golden reign,

Such, and so many, moves the warrior's train.

In bright array they seek the work of war,

Where high unfurl'd the ensign waves in air.

Shall I to Washington their praise recite?

Enough thou know'st them in the fields of fight.

Thee, first in peace and honors—we demand

The grace and glory of thy martial band.

Fam'd for thy valour, for thy virtues more,

Hear every tongue thy guardian aid implore!"

Finally, she drew upon her knowledge of history to conclude:

"One century scarce perform'd its destined round,

When Gallic powers Columbia's fury found;

And so may you, whoever dares disgrace

The land of freedom's heaven-defended race!

Fix'd are the eyes of nations on the scales,

For in their hopes Columbia's arm prevails.

Anon Britannia droops the pensive head,

> While round increase the rising hills of dead.
>
> Ah! Cruel blindness to Columbia's state!
>
> Lament thy thirst of boundless power too late.
>
> Proceed, great chief, with virtue on thy side,
>
> Thy ev'ry action let the Goddess guide.
>
> A crown, a mansion, and a throne that shine,
>
> With gold unfading, WASHINGTON! Be thine."

The war delayed the poem's arrival before Washington, as well as his reply to it. On February 28, 1776, he wrote to Phillis, "Your favour of the 26th of October did not reach my hands 'till the middle of December. Time enough, you will say, to have given an answer ere this. Granted. But a variety of important occurrences, continually interposing to distract the mind and withdraw the attention, I hope will apologize for the delay, and plead my excuse for the seeming, but not real, neglect. I thank you most sincerely for your polite notice of me, in the elegant Lines you enclosed; and however undeserving I may be of such encomium and panegyrick, the style and manner exhibit a striking proof of your great poetical Talents. In honour of which, and as a tribute justly due to you, I would have published the Poem, had I not been apprehensive, that, while I only meant to give the World this new instance of your genius, I might have incurred the imputation of Vanity. This, and nothing else, determined me not to give it place in the public Prints. If you should ever come to Cambridge, or near Head Quarters, I shall be happy to see a person so favoured by the Muses, and to whom nature has been so liberal and beneficent in her dispensations."

Phillis accepted Washington's invitation, and the two met in person in March. While there is no definitive record of what transpired between the towering general and the diminutive poet, at least one author has asserted that Wheatley's impact on Washington may have been more significant than history could immediately recognize. Writing for *History Now, The Journal of the Gilder Lehrman Institute*, James Basker observed, "Her impact on Washington, though subtle, may well have contributed to one of the most important changes in his life. Beginning shortly after his encounter with this extraordinary black poet, Washington, who had heretofore seemed no different from the typical Virginia slave owner, began to show signs of an evolving attitude about slavery and race. In 1776 he reversed an earlier decision and allowed the enlistment of black soldiers in the American army; in 1779 he supported a plan to free slaves in South Carolina if they fought on the American side; in 1786 he wrote to fellow Virginians such as John Mercer announcing his hope that the legislature would abolish slavery; and in his last will and testament Washington freed the slaves he owned…and arranged for them to be educated and trained in trades so they could support themselves."

Wheatley's poem about Washington also served an important role in her own life, for its publication brought her name, which was beginning to fade in the public memory, back into the limelight. As it turned out, it would be her last published poem until after the war ended.

The war years were difficult ones for most of the people living in the colonies, and they were especially devastating for Phillis, who lost her benefactors in quick succession. John and Mary Wheatley both died during the war, and Nathaniel never returned to America from London, so he remained unavailable to assist her. By this time, nearly half the men who had supported her work by signing the "To the PUBLICK" letter at the beginning of the book were dead, and those who were alive had more on their minds than the fate of a young poet.

Perhaps hoping to find security in the traditional roles of wife and mother, Wheatley married John Peters on April 1, 1778, but this proved to be a mistake. Peters shared neither his wife's intellect, nor her drive for success; instead, he was content to live off the gradually decreasing income from her books while also expecting her to work harder to care for him than she ever had caring for the Wheatley's. Phillis did try to continue writing, and in the Fall of 1779 she ran an advertisement in several Boston papers trying to solicit interest in publishing her work. She sent the following to Dr. Obour on May 10:

PROPOSALS,
FOR PRINTING,
BY SUBSCRIPTION
A VOLUME OF POEMS
AND LETTERS,